Strengthening Democracy in Post-conflict Northern Ireland

Maria Power

Strengthening Democracy in Post-conflict Northern Ireland:
the engagement of communities in sustaining peace

Maria Power

Five Leaves Bookshop Occasional Papers

Strengthening Democracy in Northern Ireland
by Maria Power

Published in 2015 by Five Leaves Bookshop
14a Long Row, Nottingham NG1 2DH
www.fiveleavesbookshop.co.uk

Five Leaves Bookshop Occasional Paper 3
ISBN: 978-1-910170-16-8

Designed and typeset by Five Leaves Bookshop

Printed in Great Britain

Strengthening Democracy in Northern Ireland: the engagement of communities in sustaining peace

When the Good Friday or Belfast Agreement[1] was signed in 1998, those involved believed that they 'were finally able to bring about peace in Northern Ireland'.[2] The process of implementing the accord and resolving tensions between the various political parties began and, on 7 May 2007, the Democratic Unionist Party and Sinn Fein entered government together. Nine years after the Agreement was signed, this 'historic' day was heralded by the British and Irish political classes and the media as the end of the conflict in Northern Ireland. As noted by Tony Blair in his description of that day, this achievement signalled the 'normalisation' of the region's politics to the British and Irish governments through a movement away from division:

> *Every time we set foot in Northern Ireland there were protests ... always showing how divided the politics of Northern Ireland was from that anywhere else. That day for the first time there was a protest not about Northern Ireland, but about Iraq. When I saw it, I felt that Northern Ireland had just rejoined the rest of the world.*[3]

The British and Irish governments believed that the Peace Process, with its focus on elite political settlement, was complete and it was expected that the rest of society would follow the example set by their leaders and overcome divisions to work together.

However, the resolution of conflict is not simple and, as will be demonstrated later in this essay, Northern Ireland is not peaceful. Now that the political structures have been implemented, emphasis needs to be placed upon relationships between communities and peace-building[4] work focused on dealing with the sectarian divisions within society is required. Senator George Mitchell's analysis of Northern Irish society illustrates this:

> It's a deeply divided society, it continues that way. While one can agree on political and security measures, it takes a very long time, generations perhaps, to change people's hearts and minds. So while this is a very important step, no-one should think that trust and love is going to be breaking out tomorrow between the two communities in Northern Ireland. That will take a long time.[5]

Organisations aimed at peace building in Northern Ireland have been in existence as long as the conflict itself. Ranging from the widely-reported demonstrations organised by the Peace People in the mid-1970s to the quiet work of cross-community groups in local areas, those involved have sought to present an alternative vision to the polarisation that has dominated Northern Irish politics since partition in 1921. These schemes functioned by focusing on relationships between communities and operated in both middle and working-class areas. They worked towards an improvement in community relations by enabling participants to understand the perspective of the 'other' community and accept that differences are not threatening. Such grassroots engagement with issues connected to community relations is crucial because, as we shall see, it has the potential to promote political stability and enable the development of democracy. Thus, if we are to fully comprehend the peace process in Northern Ireland, the work of peace-building organisations and their role and place within society needs to be understood and analysed.[6]

The Political Context

The accord reached at Stormont was certainly significant, not least for the participation of republicans in the process eventually leading to the Democratic Unionist Party and Sinn Fein agreeing to work together in government in 2007 but whether it finally brought peace is, as the negotiations leading up to the 2014 Stormont House Agreement[7] demonstrate, highly debatable. The signing of the Agreement and subsequent negotiations leading to the Hillsborough Agreement of 2010, created political structures based upon a revised form of consociationalism[8] in Northern Ireland.[9] The benefits of such an arrangement for areas of conflict have been described thus: 'The consociationalist argument is that particularly in certain contexts — deeply divided societies, where divisions are longstanding and when there is intra-group violence — it is more realistic to accept that different groups will continue to exist than to seek the "deconstruction" of group ties.'[10]

The Agreement enabled Northern Ireland to remain part of the United Kingdom as long as the majority consented, provided for an all-Ireland dimension and established a Northern Ireland Assembly elected by proportional representation and a power-sharing Executive, the membership of which would be based upon the various political parties' electoral success. These new institutions were predicated upon the conclusion that the conflict in Northern Ireland was based upon ethno-national rather than economic concerns.[11] But as Stefan Wolff argued, 'defining the Northern Ireland conflict ... as an ethno-national one has important implications for its analysis and for the analysis of attempts to settle it.'[12] Consequently, a form of consociationalism was seen as the solution. The situation would be resolved if the divisions that existed within society were acknowledged and elite-level structures were created that would enable the political accommodation of the ethno-national groups, resulting in 'stability, fairness and democracy'.[13] The Agreement, it was argued by John McGarry and Brendan O'Leary, did just this.

Stability has been brought to Northern Ireland through the Agreement's role in the cessation of paramilitary violence and decommissioning of weapons by the participant's reaffirmation of 'their commitment to the total disarmament of all paramilitary organisations.'[14] This has seen both republican and loyalist paramilitaries put their weapons 'beyond use' leaving 'relatively little prospect of a significant resurgence in political violence.'[15] Thus, according to McGarry and O'Leary, since 1994, violence has declined by 80 per cent and 'Belfast [is] the world's second safest city for crime,' producing a 'peace dividend' that has seen employment rates, until the recent financial crisis struck, rise.[16] Furthermore, whilst not privileging identities over one another, the Agreement provided safeguards for the communities involved by enabling them 'to be protected whether they are majorities or minorities, and whether sovereignty lies with the United Kingdom or the Republic.'[17] Finally, consociationalists believe that democracy has been achieved: those elected to office are 'dependent on democratic support, and voters are free to withhold that support and to vote for other parties instead.'[18] The Agreement, according to this line of reasoning, has therefore facilitated a cessation of the conflict in Northern Ireland by not only addressing the issue of conflict management but also that of resolution through its focus upon equality issues as well as political structures. Thus, the Agreement and subsequent political developments 'had the potential to bring closure to the conflict.'[19]

But, as Rupert Taylor argues, 'far more is required for conflict resolution than consociationalists presume.'[20] Such thoughts are echoed by Ian O'Flynn who states 'it is easier to manage conflict than try to resolve it.'[21] At present, the elite-level political system engrains political identities, allowing little room for alternatives to develop. Through the political structures implemented, which focus upon acknowledging and engraining difference, 'it copper-fastened the importance of groups and in doing so denied not only the heterogeneous nature of Northern Irish society but also the assembly of diverse voices within groups.'[22] However, in order for the conflict to be resolved in Northern Ireland, something more than a consociationalist system is needed, especially as this arrangement does not address the sectarianism which provided the impetus for the conflict and continues to fuel sporadic crime.[23]

Relationships between the communities, at a grassroots as well as elite level, need to be ameliorated through peace building rather than managed through complex political arrangements as is currently the case. The Agreement has gone some way towards doing this as it addresses some of the key structural problems, such as inequality, that were one of the causes of conflict. But, as a consequence of the Agreement's focus on ethno-nationalism, it fails to place enough emphasis upon the part that conflicted relationships, division and sectarianism have played in creating tensions between the two communities. This has been compounded by the development of a governmental policy regarding the issue of peace building or community relations through A Shared Future (launched in 2005), the Programme for Sharing, Cohesion and Integration (launched in 2010), and Together: Building a United Community (launched in 2013).[24]

Peace-building policies focused on improving community relations became a victim of the uncertainty surrounding devolved government and according to Duncan Morrow, the former Chief Executive of the Community Relations Council, 'devolved government did not like A Shared Future. The fact it was enacted under a British direct rule government was enough to make it an object of suspicion. But agreeing an alternative has proved a hard ask.'[25] These government policies raise many questions regarding issues such as communal separation, shared housing and integrated education but place them within a long-term framework rather than viewing them as a means to solve pressing problems. But as Joseph Ruane and Jennifer Todd suggest 'if we take seriously the potential and the danger of current processes of cultural change, then these aims are as important as the immediate tasks of tackling interface violence and sectarian incidents. Indeed without programmes that deal with these strategic aims, the immediate problems will continue to be reproduced.'[26] For the critics of the consociationalist approach, this is a demonstration of its failure to understand the basic nature of the conflict and the need for the ethno-nationalism that forms the core of this approach to be eroded before the Northern Irish conflict can be fully resolved.[27] In order for a peace process to be successful and more importantly sustainable, the problems, such as communal division, relating to the conflict must be addressed coherently rather than hoping the example of cooperation at the elite level will eventually trickle down to the grassroots.[28]

However, peace building in Northern Irish society is hindered by a number of factors. The narrow definition of peace upon which the process in Northern Ireland has been brokered has implications for its development. In most conflict situations, the 'termination of violent acts is often equated with the state of peace'.[29] This issue has been articulated thus:

> In 1999, at a seminar on peacemaking and preventative diplomacy sponsored by the UN Institute for Training and Research, a participant identified two types of peace: the 'no more shooting type' and the 'no more need for shooting type'. The remark captured an essential distinction governing the resolution of conflicts, between ensuring the minimal conditions for peace — ending the fighting between armed factions or between insurgents and the state — and building peace over the long term, by establishing stable polities that process and deal with conflict without recourse to violence. This latter effort involves an attempt to address at least some of the conditions that led to the conflict in the first place.[30]

In Northern Ireland, the dramatic fall in troubles-related deaths[31] has been viewed as an end to conflict.[32] But, conflict continues by other means. Instances of sectarian criminal damage have rise by 15% in the period between 2008/9 and 2009/10 although at 573, this figure is still lower than the 677 incidents reported in 2005/6, whilst the most recent figures suggest that the numbers of such attacks have increased in the past year.[33] Crime motivated by sectarianism rose by 25% between 2008 and 2009[34] with 1284 crimes being reported in 2013/14.[35] The numbers of racially motivated incidents are steadily multiplying with 691 racist crimes being reported in 2013/14 compared to 470 in 2012/13.[36] Paramilitary-style shootings have increased from 16 in 2008 to 30 in 2011[37] but this figure is still half of what it was in 2005. In addition, the numbers of paramilitary-style assaults doubled from 40 in 2008 to 81 in 2009,[38] the figure rising to 46 in 2011.[39]

There is evidence to suggest that Northern Ireland has become more segregated since 1998: the number of peace lines maintained by the Northern Irish Office has grown from 37 in October 2006 to 59 in November 2012.[40] In addition, in 2010 the Community Relations Council listed 88 segregation and security barriers in Belfast alone,[41] with this figure rising to 99 in 2014;[42] and a successful application was made to Derry City Council to erect a new interface at Lisnagelvin in March 2011.[43] According to the Northern Irish Justice Minister, David Ford, 'These walls, fences and gates are daily reminders that, despite the political progress we have made over the last decade, we still have a huge challenge ahead to break down the mistrust and separation that exists within our community.'[44] Suggestions have been made on their removal, but such a process would take at least five years to complete, requiring the cooperation and support of local communities and the government.[45]

Much social or public housing (which was the epicentre of most of the conflict's violence) remains segregated. The 2001 Census suggested that 70% of social housing tenants live in areas that are at least 90% Catholic or Protestant,[46] with this figure increasing to 93% in the 2011 Census.[47] In addition, 37% of the Northern

Irish population live in segregated areas[48] and in 2011/12, 148 people asked for housing transfers due to intimidation compared to 62 in 2005/6.[49] Finally, whilst in 2012, 70% of people said they would send their child to an integrated school, only 6.8% actually did. This lack of integration in education is somewhat softened by a trend that has emerged for Catholic parents to send their children to controlled or state schools, whilst a smaller proportion of Protestants are sending theirs to maintained or Catholic schools.[50]

As well as their impact upon community relations in Northern Ireland, these elements of the conflict have financial implications for the region. Research by Deloitte and Touche found that 'the issues of segregation and conflict continue to influence policy decisions, public service provision and hence resource allocation' with the cost of division being estimated at £1.5 billion annually.[51] Thus, employment that encourages and enables communities to work together or share resources would also be financially beneficial for the region.

Despite this, popular perceptions of the strength of community relations have improved in the years since the Agreement (although they have fluctuated mainly as a consequence of events, such as the Holy Cross protests in 2001). In 1996, prior to the Agreement being signed, a social attitudes survey demonstrated that 43% of the population thought that relationships between Protestants and Catholics would be improved in five years time.[52] By 2009, these figures stood at 68% for Catholics, 56% for Protestants and 67% for those with no religion, whilst in 2012 these figures stood at 52% for both Catholics and Protestants.[53] These figures are still lower than they were at their peaks in 1995, 1999 and 2007.[54] Furthermore, the disparity between Catholics, Protestants, and those with no religion, demonstrates that a gulf still exists between the communities in Northern Ireland regarding their attitudes to the normalisation of society. As Paula Devine and others note, this could raise questions about their belief in the efficacy of the peace process:

> *There is little room for complacency. The most recent results*
> *appear to indicate that respondents have some concern that*
> *relations between the two main communities have become as*
> *good as they can get and that further improvement is unlikely*
> *— or perhaps undesirable.*[55]

Consequently, although it has been argued, in particular by McGarry and O'Leary, that stability and democracy have been brought to the region, such statistics demonstrate that despite the fact that the devolved institutions provided by the Agreement are now working, Northern Irish society is not peaceful. The sectarianism that motivated the conflict still remains. It now manifests itself through crime rather than terrorist activities and needs to be dealt with constructively in a way that will eventually allow the 'no more need for shooting' type of peace to emerge and strengthen the stability brought by the Agreement and ensuring the continuation of democracy.

The contribution of Peace Building to Northern Irish Society

Critiques of the nature of the Agreement and the political settlement in Northern Ireland indicate that additional structures and support need to be implemented in order to underpin the start made in 1998. In the years immediately after the Agreement, some academics and commentators called for public policies to be created which would promote social integration. For instance, Rick Wilford and Robin Wilson argued that 'If political stability is to be won, policy needs to change from "consociationalism" and crisis-management and towards a focus on integration and a strategic commitment to the emergence of a civil society.'[56] Such an idea, it was argued, would lead to the dilution of ethno-national identities in Northern Ireland and create cross-cutting identities, encouraging people to think beyond the politics of the conflict. Whilst embedding 'bread and butter' issues into the politics of the region is one of the ultimate goals of a peace process, the rate at which this should be done and the methods that need to be employed are debateable. This is especially true of Northern Ireland where:

> *The legacy of conflict and violence is a long one. This is especially true in those areas where conflict was most acute. Whereas people living in districts where conflict was an unusual, sporadic or distant experience have often embraced the benefits of peace with relief, trust is not easily won in the face of recent memory of bereavement, anger and fear.*[57]

Such problems are not easily solved and need to be addressed at a local as well as national level. Thus instead of pursuing a policy of integration, in order for the progress towards democracy and stability brought by the restoration of devolved government to be sustained, relationships at the grassroots need to be reconciled and developed. Peace processes stand a better chance of success if the whole of society, rather than just the elite level, is involved and one of the main ways to engage people is through forms of peace-building activity.[58] Through such work, stability and democratic participation can be improved if relationships between communities are encouraged by the forms of contact and work, such as integrated education and faith-based encounters.[59] Through such engagements people are encouraged 'to make a genuine effort to understand the force of [the other community's] views' and 'to reflect seriously on what they have to say, rather than simply treating them as obstacles or enemies'[60] or indeed pretending that they do not exist. However, rather than creating a single public identity for a region that has suffered ethnic conflict,[61] such schemes focus on relationships, removing the fear and mistrust that in many areas helped to generate the conflict. As John Paul Lederach argues, 'it is perhaps self-evident but oft-neglected that *relationship* is the basis of the conflict and its long-term solution. ... Reconciliation is not pursued by those seeking innovative ways to disengage or minimize the conflicting groups' affiliations, but instead is built upon mechanisms that engage the sides of a conflict with each other as humans-in-relationship.'[62] Such work has the potential to improve community relations thereby negating the causes of the conflict and its violence, as well as dealing with the consequences without erasing people's ethnic identities.

In the years leading up to the Agreement and its immediate aftermath, the role of civil society (the main arena through which grassroots peace-building takes place) in the Northern Irish peace process attracted some attention.[63] There was a tendency in this literature, as in the governmental policy that promotes this work, to see the political process and civil society as two parallel structures which worked alongside each other rather than with one another. So, for example, David Bloomfield rightly commented that in Northern Ireland:

> ... it is noteworthy that two practical approaches exist simultaneously, and appear to operate in different areas of the conflict and to address different concerns, rather than alternating with each other either on the same parts of the conflict or on the conflict as a whole.[64]

However, the negotiations leading up to the Agreement demonstrated the centrality that the peace-building or community relations sector had in conflict resolution.[65] In the immediate aftermath of this, civil society organisations offered mass support to political processes through the 'yes' campaign.[66] The Agreement also contained 'a framework within which the underlying conditions of the conflict can be addressed ... as a framework for addressing the deeper roots of division, its goal is to generate and channel wide-ranging social changes to secure reconciliation within Northern Ireland and on the island of Ireland.'[67] The means through which such an aim might be realised is one of the main goals of peace building.

The potential for such peace-building work to contribute to the continuation of peace processes post-Agreement through its focus on relationships has been demonstrated by Ashutosh Varshney.[68] This study shows that inter-communal contact holds the key to the resolution of conflict and more importantly the maintenance of peace by reducing the risk of violence and further polarisation whilst improving community relationships. Whilst everyday contact[69] and associational contact[70] are both important to promoting peace, associational contact is 'sturdier' in its ability to maintain calm in conflict situations. Thus, the pre-existence of such associational contact means that any conflict which occurs can be dealt with peacefully and through negotiation rather than erupting into violence. Where such networks of engagement exist, 'tensions and conflicts were regulated and managed; where they were missing, communal identities led to endemic and ghastly violence.'[71] Associational contact acts as a check on politicians who wish to promote an agenda that would damage relationships. This is because 'vigorous associational life, if inter-communal, acts as a serious constraint on the polarizing strategies of political elites.'[72]

Varshney presents two reasons for this: firstly, such inter-communal contact promotes ease of communication as the trust which is a prerequisite for peace is already present. Secondly, associational contact provides an understanding of points of common concern within a community and represents its interests. These concerns can be economic, social or cultural, for example, but they provide a stronger point of reference than everyday interactions thereby strengthening relationships and providing a powerful hindrance for violence as everyone 'would suffer losses from a communal split fight for their turf.'[73]

At present, current levels of segregation in Northern Ireland prevent associational contact from operating in the same way. Consequently, grassroots peace building has a role to play in encouraging such associational contact by facilitating and mediating communication. By encountering one another in the associational form encouraged by the peace building , those involved can reduce 'othering' and enable people to work together on points of common concern without a loss of their own identities to a single public identity. Furthermore, this form of associational engagement can increase stability within previously volatile areas as it promotes the acceptance of the interdependence of different communities.

Peace building also contributes to the strengthening and maintenance of democracy as a result of its concentration upon the whole of society rather than just the elite political class. Such a focus is vital because, as Michael Walzer notes, 'deepening democracy is the responsibility of everyone in society, not simply the responsibility of politicians.'[74] It enables people to join in this process in two key ways: it exposes participants to alternative points of view to their own and it provides members of divided communities with a means to work together to have their needs and concerns addressed through their political structures rather than resorting to violence as has previously been the case.

Debate and discussion with those that hold divergent points of view is crucial to democracy. This is especially true in areas where there is ethnic tension: 'if people only engage in discussion and debate with members of their own ethnic group, they may view every issue as an ethnic issue and hence fail to recognise the importance to democracy of exposing themselves to alternative views.'[75] Providing a forum through which people can encounter alternate points of view, peace-building organisations support the democratic process by allowing participants to become fully informed when making political decisions regarding, for example, voting choices. Given the need to remove ethnicity as a source of conflict in Northern Ireland, peace building has a significant contribution to make as it enables people to 'engage in discussion and debate' around issues of contention with the support, such as mediation and facilitation, that is necessary to avoid further conflict.

The importance of peace building to the maintenance of democracy is further increased by the divisions within Northern

Irish society: unless people are willing to communicate with those that oppose them, their exclusivist identities will be reinforced and leading to 'maximalist or uncompromising demands'[76] being made. Such behaviour will move society away from the form of accommodation practiced at the elite political level and hinder the continuation of the process begun with the 1998 Agreement.

Peace building also offers people a political voice and access to those that have been disenfranchised by the violent and polarised nature of conflict, such as women, thereby promoting the 'maintenance of democracy through the peaceful articulation of the interests of all sections of the community.'[77] Thus,

> *Just as it is possible to create institutions that facilitate power sharing between the representatives of different ethnic groups, it is possible to create institutions that facilitate participation and deliberation between ordinary people, both within and across different ethnic groups, and that enable them to effectively channel their views and opinions to government.*[78]

The creation of such organisations encourages democratic engagement beyond the political elites, promoting the idea that engagement with those from the 'other' community can be an empowering rather than disempowering process. The importance of the good or improved relationships developed between different groups through this work to this process is clear. It helps society as a whole to move beyond the polarised nature of politics by creating new cross-community cleavages. But possibly more importantly, as has been shown in other conflict zones, 'the local organs of the state function better when there are robust links [between different ethnic groups] in civic life ... An attempt to rebuild or strengthen civic links between [such groups] is a method that, although indirect, is more effective in keeping the state accountable for the life of its citizens.'[79]

This is a step towards the 'normalisation' of Northern Irish politics and an acceleration of the biodegradation of ethnic politics that consociationalists hope will occur. Moreover, as past experience has demonstrated, the grassroots and mid-range leaderships of such organisations have the ability to represent the views of their members to the top-level leaderships. As stated earlier, such behaviour existed during the negotiations leading to the Agreement, so it would be expected that peace-building organisations would continue to operate in the same manner post-accord and act as a support to the democratic institutions by enabling people to hold their political representatives to account and to have their views represented beyond the polling booth.

Peace-building work has come under a great deal of scrutiny and criticism from, for example, academics and the media. These critiques range from suggestions that it simply is not needed as the political violence has ceased, to those that argue that such work actually prevents Northern Irish society from moving on and becoming 'normal'. This, when combined with the fact that there is no definitive way of measuring the impact and effectiveness of this work, means that its usefulness will always be under question. According to its critics, the problem primarily lies in the lack of debate surrounding it:

> One view (perhaps the prevailing one during the 1980s–90s), that the mere existence of the P/CRO [peace and conflict-resolution organisations] sector has been beneficial regardless of any empirically definable achievements, is unimpressive. It epitomises the woolly liberalism and well-meaning but ultimately ineffectual culture for which the sector has rightly been criticised. Given the amount of public money that has been poured into the P/CRO 'industry' over the last 30 years, its defenders will have to come up with more than a 'better than nothing' advocacy to justify its existence.[80]

Added to this is the argument that peace-building work is effectively superfluous to the needs of Northern Irish society. The numbers of conflict-related deaths have fallen dramatically and there is now an acceptable level of violence within the region. According to this reasoning, the evidence regarding divisions in society is impressionistic and can easily be explained away.[81] Indeed, such critics point out that the politics of the peace process focused upon the realpolitik and was spurred on by moments of violence rather than the work of peace-building organisations and their ideologies.[82] Closely linked to this is the notion that within Northern Ireland a self-perpetuating 'peace industry' exists which justifies itself in terms of its contribution to the peace process.

> *Northern Ireland's dirty little secret is that there is an entire tranche of the population, from euphemistic "community workers", to quangocrats pocketing hundred-thousand pay packets, who rely on Northern Ireland remaining different and on the distant shadow of the gunman and the occasional bomber and riot for their livelihood.[83]*

This 'industry' amounts to £1 billion per annum, is Northern Ireland's largest employer and creates a self-sustaining cycle that 'lowers expectations and sends out negative messages'.[84]

This communalisation and professionalization of peace building has the potential to disenfranchise the very people that it is supposed to help by stifling the creativity and spontaneity that is inherent in this form of grassroots action.[85] According to this critique, the economic development of the region is being hindered as the peace industry stifles the inward investment that is vital for the economic rejuvenation needed to tackle the socio-economic depravation that fuels conflict to occur. In addition to the criticisms surrounding the existence of peace-building organisations, the work that they undertake has also been the subject of unfavourable commentary. This focuses upon the methods employed and the subjects that are broached. During the conflict in Northern Ireland, suspicion and mistrust dominated everyday interactions, conversation focused on topics regarded as safe. Work aimed at improving relationships between the two communities is often regarded as perpetuating this convention. Thus, those involved are not encouraged to address the 'contentious' issues, a practice which endorses avoidance and 'denial', increasing misunderstandings between those involved and thereby perpetuating conflict.

It is often suggested that this work is dominated by middle-class 'do-gooders', rather than the working classes who were most directly affected by the conflict. Despite this, there is a need to understand more clearly the forms that peace building has taken in Northern Ireland.

As events, such as the 2012–13 Belfast Flag Protests and the negotiations leading up to the 2014 Stormont House Agreement show, the conflict in Northern Ireland, whilst not as violent as it once was, still has the potential to erupt. Such latent conflict also has the power to disrupt the democratic processes that were the main achievement of the 1998 Agreement. Northern Irish society now needs to deal with the legacy of the conflict, a major element of which was the breakdown in relationships between communities. Despite its issues, peace building has a great deal to offer post-conflict societies, but patience and perseverance are required to ensure its success.

Notes

1. Hereafter known as 'the Agreement', see http://www.nio.gov.uk/agreement.pdf (accessed 11 July 2010).

2. J Powell, *Great Hatred, Little Room: Making Peace in Northern Ireland*, (London, 2008), p. 309.

3. T Blair, *A Journey*, (London, 2010), p. 199.

4. One of the issues regarding the study of peace building, civil society and conflict transformation in Northern Ireland is the lack of agreed definition of any of the terms. For a full discussion of this issue see S Buchanan, 'Examining the Peacebuilding Policy Framework of the Irish and British Governments' in M Power (ed.), *Building Peace in Northern Ireland*, (Liverpool, 2011), pp. 172-190.

5. Senator George Mitchell, speaking on 26 March 2007, cited in J McGarry and B O'Leary, 'Power shared after the deaths of thousands', R Taylor (ed.), *Consociational Theory: McGarry and O'Leary and the Northern Ireland Conflict*, (Abingdon, 2009), pp. 15-84, 15.

6. Such forms of peace-building work within civil society in Northern Ireland, whilst they do not make up all of civil society or indeed even adhere to the ethos of some of it, they do have a crucial role to play in the peace process: For a discussion of the negative impact that some elements of civil society can have on peace processes see M Cox, *Social Capital and Peace building: Creating and resolving conflict with trust and social networks*, (Oxford, 2009).

7. This Agreement dealt with a number of issues including: the past, flags, and parades, as well as welfare and fiscal reform, see https://www.gov.uk/government/publications/the-stormont-house-agreement, (accessed 13 January 2015).

8. Tonge defines the classic features of consociationalism as power sharing, proportionality in government, mutual vetoes and bloc autonomy. J Tonge, *Northern Ireland*, (Cambridge, 2006), p. 26. See also D L Horowitz, 'Explaining the Northern Ireland Agreement: the sources of an unlikely constitutional consensus', *British Journal of Political Science*, 2002, vol. 32, pp. 193-220, 194.

9. J McGarry and B O'Leary, *The Northern Ireland Conflict: Consociational Engagements*, (Oxford, 2004), pp. 262-3.

10. J McGarry, 'Political Settlements in Northern Ireland and South Africa', *Political Studies*, 1998, vol. 46, no. 5, pp. 853-870, 860.

11. J McGarry and B O'Leary, *The Politics of Antagonism: Understanding Northern Ireland*, (London, 1996), 4 and *Explaining Northern Ireland: Broken Images*, (Oxford, 1995), p. 306.

12. S Wolff, 'From Sunningdale to Belfast, 1973-98', Jorg Neuheiser and Stefan Wolff, *Peace at Last? The Impact of the Good Friday Agreement on Northern Ireland*, (Oxford, 2002), pp. 1-24, 1.

13. McGarry and O'Leary, 'Power shared after the deaths of thousands', p. 47. This article provides a full outline of the case for the success of the Agreement.

14. The Agreement on Decommissioning.

15. McGarry and O'Leary, 'Power Shared after the deaths of thousands', p. 47.

16. Ibid.

17. McGarry and O'Leary, *The Northern Ireland Conflict*, p. 280.

18. McGarry and O'Leary, 'Power Shared after the deaths of thousands', p. 80.

19. Tonge, *Northern Ireland*, p. 189.

20. R Taylor, 'The injustice of a consociational solution to Northern Ireland', Taylor (ed.), *Consociational Theory*, pp. 309-329, 310.

21. I O'Flynn, 'Progressive integration (and accommodation too)', Taylor (ed.), *Consociational Theory*, pp. 264-278, 278.

22. P Shirlow and B Murtagh, *Belfast: Segregation, Violence and the City*, (London, 2006), p. 5.

23. *Belfast Newsletter*, 9 March 2011 or *Belfast Media*, 8 March 2011, http://www.belfastmedia.com/home_article.php?ID=2333, (accessed 16 March 2011).

24. *A Shared Future – Policy and Strategic Framework for Good Relations*, (Belfast, 2005), http://www.ofmdfmni.gov.uk/index/ equality/community-relations/a-shared-future-strategy.htm (accessed 31 January 2011)and *Programme For Cohesion, Sharing And Integration* (Belfast, 2010), http://www.nidirect.gov.uk/reformatted_final_print_version_csi_- _26.07.10.pdf (accessed 31 January 2011) and *Together: Building a*

United Community, (Belfast, 2013), http://www.ofmdfmni.gov.uk/
together-building-a-united-community-strategy.pdf (accessed 13
January 2015).

25. *Irish Times*, 25 October 2010. See also P Devine, Shared and Safe?
An update on Good Relations policy and public attitudes', *Ark
Research Update*, no. 90, March 2014, http://www.ark.ac.uk/
publications/updates/Update90.pdf, (accessed 13 January 2015).

26. J Todd and J Ruane, *From 'A Shared Future' to 'Cohesion, Sharing
and Integration': An Analysis of Northern Ireland's Policy Framework
Documents*, (York, 2010), p. 17.

27. For an example of this argument see: R Taylor, 'Northern Ireland:
Consociation or Social Transformation?', J McGarry, (ed.), *Northern
Ireland and the Divided World, Post-Agreement Northern Ireland in
Comparative Perspective*, (Oxford, 2001), pp. 37-52.

28. See for example, McGarry and O'Leary, 'Power shared after the
deaths of thousands', p. 68.

29. O Ramsbotham, 'The Analysis of Protracted Social Conflict: a
tribute to Edward Azar', *Review of International Studies*, 2005,
vol. 31, no. 1, pp. 109-126, 114.

30. C J Arnson and D Azpuru, 'From Peace to Democratization:
Lessons from Central America', J Darby and R MacGinty (eds.),
Contemporary Peacemaking: Conflict, Violence and Peace Processes,
(Basingstoke, 2003), pp. 197-211, 197.

31. In 2014, there were 4 Troubles-related deaths compared to 253 in
1989-91, CAIN, 'Draft List of Deaths Related to the Conflict in
2014', http://cain.ulst.ac.uk/issues/violence/deaths2014draft.htm,
(accessed 13 January 2015). Troubles-related deaths are those that
can be directly attributed to the political conflict.

32. For example, in a 2011 broadcast of 'Thinking Allowed' on BBC
Radio 4, Laurie Taylor commented that most of his listeners would
be surprised to hear that paramilitary punishment beatings were
still a feature of life in West Belfast. 'Thinking Allowed' broadcast
19 January 2011, http://www.bbc.co.uk/iplayer/console/b00xhj80/
Thinking_Allowed_19_01_2011, (accessed 31 January 2011).

33. Police Service of Northern Ireland, *Trends in Hate Motivated
Incidents and Crime Recorded by the Police in Northern Ireland
2004/05 to 2013/14*, (Belfast, 2014), http://www.psni.police.uk/

hate_motivated_incidents_and_crimes_in_northern_ireland_2004-05_to_2013-14.pdf, (accessed 13 January 2015), p. 12.

34. Office of the First Minister and Deputy First Minister, *Good Relations Indicators 2010 Update*, (Belfast, January 2011) http://www.ofmdfmni.gov.uk/index/equality/equalityresearch/ research-publications/gr-pubs.htm (accessed 31 January 2011), Priority Outcome 1.

35. PSNI, *Trends in Hate Motivated Incidents and Crime Recorded by the Police in Northern Ireland*, p. 9.

36. Ibid.

37. Office of the First Minister and Deputy First Minister, *Good Relations Indicators – 2012 Update*, (Belfast, January 2013), http://www.ofmdfmni.gov.uk/gr-pubs, (accessed 13 January 2015), Priority Outcome 3.

38. OFMDFM, *Good Relations Indicators 2010 Update*, Priority Outcome 3. For a discussion of the causes of such attacks and the increases see H Hamill, *The Hoods: Crime and Punishment in Belfast: Crime and Punishment in West Belfast*, (New Jersey, 2010).

39. OFMDFM, *Good Relations Indicators 2012 Update*, Priority Outcome 3.

40. These are located in Belfast, Derry, Portadown and Lurgan. Priority Outcome 3 lists this figure as 59 for November 2012 and comments that 'No new peace walls have been erected since 2008. The increase in numbers to 59 is due to a re-categorisation of some structures, for example the gates on Derry City walls were previously counted as 1 structure, they are now counted as 7. The Department of Justice became responsible for the 59 structures in April 2010, and lead on PfG commitment number 68 to actively seek local agreement to reduce the number of peace walls.' Ibid.

41. Such barriers include (but are not limited to) physical structures such as walls and fences, security gates designed to enable areas to be closed off and buffer zones of derelict land or brownfield sites at an interface or at the boundary of a marked residential area. Community Relations Council, *Towards Sustainable Security: Interface Barriers and the Legacy of Segregation in Belfast*, (Belfast, 2008). 11-20. http://www.conflictresearch.org.uk/cms/images/ stories/daniel/pdfs/iwg%20publication2.pdf (accessed 7 July 2010).

42. Paul Nolan, *Northern Ireland Peace Monitoring Report*, no. 3, (Belfast, March 2014), http://www.community-relations.org.uk/wp-content/uploads/2013/11/Peace-Monitoring-Report-2014.pdf, (accessed 13 January 2015), p. 67.

43. *Belfast Telegraph*, 4 March 2011.

44. David Ford speaking on 16 February 2011, Community Relations Council, 'Peacelines remain obstacle to a shared future', http://www.community-relations.org.uk/about-us/news/item/671/peacelines-remain-obstacle-to-shared-future-ford/, (accessed 17 February 2011).

45. T Macauley, *A Process for Removing Interface Barriers: A discussion paper proposing a five phase process for the removal of 'peace walls' in Northern Ireland*, (Belfast, 2008). http://cain.ulst.ac.uk/issues/segregat/docs/macaulay200708.pdf (accessed 7 July 2010).

46. Equality Commission for Northern Ireland, *Statement on Key Inequalities in Northern Ireland*, (Belfast, 2007), http://www.equalityni.org/archive/pdf/Keyinequalities(F)1107.pdf, (accessed 31 January 2011), p. 21.

47. Nolan, *Northern Ireland Peace Monitoring Report*, no. 3, p. 114.

48. Ibid., p. 115.

49. *Good Relations Indicators 2012 Update*, Priority Outcome 5.

50. Ibid., Priority Outcome 4. The reasons for this are more complex than an unwillingness to educate children together and probably relate more closely to the educational aspirations of parents for their children.

51. Deloitte, *Research into the financial cost of the divide in Northern Ireland*, (April 2007), p. 88.

52. Joanne Hughes and Paul Carmichael, 'Community Relations in Northern Ireland: Attitudes to Contact and Integration' in G Robinson, D Heenan, A M Gray and K Thompson (eds.), *Social Attitudes in Northern Ireland: The Seventh Report*, (Aldershot, 1998). For an analysis of attitudes in the middle of this period see *The Guardian*, 4 January 2002.

53. Duncan Morrow, Gillian Robinson, and Lizanne Dowds, 'The Long View of Community Relations in Northern Ireland: 1989-2012', *Ark*

Research Update, no. 87, (May 2014) http://www.ark.ac.uk/publications/updates/update87.pdf, (accessed 13 January 2015).

54. P Devine, G Kelly, and G Robinson, 'An age of change? Community Relations in Northern Ireland', *Ark Research Update*, no. 72, January 2011, http://www.ark.ac.uk/publications/updates/update72.pdf (accessed 13 January 2015), p. 3.

55. Ibid., p. 4.

56. R Wilson and R Wilford, 'Northern Ireland: a route to stability?', Policy paper commissioned by the Economic and Social Research Council, (2003).

57. Community Relations Council, *Towards Sustainable Security*, p. 3.

58. J P Lederach, *Building Peace: Sustainable Reconciliation in Divided Societies*, (Washington DC, 1997).

59. See Power (ed.), *Building Peace in Northern Ireland*.

60. O'Flynn, 'Progressive integration (and accommodation too)', p. 270.

61. McGarry and O'Leary, 'Power shared after deaths of thousands'.

62. Lederach, *Building Peace*, p. 26.

63. D Bloomfield, *Peacemaking Strategies in Northern Ireland: Building Complementarity in Conflict Management Theory*, (Basingstoke, 1997), S Byrne, 'Consociational and Civic Society Approaches to Peace building in Northern Ireland', *Journal of Peace Research*, 2001, vol. 38, no. 3, pp. 327-352, F Cochrane and S Dunn, *People Power? The role of the voluntary and community sector in the Northern Ireland Conflict*, (Cork, 2002), P Dixon, 'Paths to Peace in Northern Ireland (I): Civil society and consociational approaches', *Democratization*, 1997, vol. 4, no.2, pp. 1-27 and A Guelke, 'Civil Society and the Northern Irish Peace Process', *Voluntas*, 2003, vol. 3, no. 1, pp. 61-78.

64. Bloomfield, *Peacemaking Strategies in Northern Ireland*, p. 85.

65. F Cochrane and S Dunn, 'Peace and Conflict Resolution Organisations in Northern Ireland' in B Gidron, S N Katz, Y Hasenfeld (Eds.) *Mobilizing for Peace: Conflict Resolution in Northern Ireland, Israel/Palestine, and South Africa* (Oxford, 2005) pp. 151-71, 170. The Northern Ireland Women's Coalition's participation in the negotiations were emblematic of this. see C Murtagh, 'A Transient Transition: The Cultural and Institutional

Obstacles Impeding the Northern Ireland Women's Coalition in its Progression from Informal to Formal Politics', *Irish Political Studies*, (2008),vol. 23, no. 1, pp. 21-40.

66. R A Couto, 'The Third Sector and Civil Society: The Case of the "YES" Campaign in Northern Ireland', *Voluntas: International Journal of Voluntary and Nonprofit Organizations*, (2001), Vol. 12, No. 3, pp. 221-238.

67. J Ruane and J Todd, 'The Belfast Agreement: Context, Content and Consequences', J Ruane and J Todd, (eds.), *After the Good Friday Agreement: Analysing Political Change in Northern Ireland*, (Dublin, 1999), pp. 1-29, 17.

68. A Varshney, *Ethnic Conflict and Civic Life: Hindus and Muslims in India*, (New Haven, 2002). Although the focus of this study is on India, the form of sectarian division that he explores contains useful ideas regarding the importance of contact for peace building.

69. Defined as 'routine interactions of life as Hindu and Muslim families visiting each other, eating together often enough, jointly participating in festivals, and allowing their children to play together'. Ibid., p. 3.

70. Some examples are 'Business associations, professional organisations, trade unions and cadre-based poitical parties', ibid.

71. Ibid., p. 9.

72. Ibid., p. 4.

73. Ibid., p. 11.

74. I O'Flynn and D Russell, 'Deepening Democracy: the role of civil society', K Cordell and S Wolff (eds.), *The Routledge Handbook of Ethnic Conflict*, (Oxford, 2011), pp. 225-35, 231 paraphrasing M Walzer, *Politics and Passion: Towards a more egalitarian liberalism*, (New Haven, 2004), p. 83.

75. Ibid., p. 229.

76. Ibid., p. 230.

77. Westmoreland General Meeting, *Preparing for Peace — by asking the experts to analyse war*, (Westmoreland, 2005), p. 36.

78. O'Flynn and Russell, 'Deepening Democracy', pp. 226-7.

79. Varshney, *Ethnic Conflict and Civic Life*, p. 289.

80. F Cochrane, 'Unsung Heroes or Muddle-Headed Peaceniks? A Profile and Assessment of NGO Conflict Resolution Activity in the Northern Ireland 'Peace Process'', *Irish Studies in International Affairs*, (2001), Vol. 12, pp. 97-112, 108.

81. McGarry and O'Leary, 'Power shared after deaths of thousands', pp. 47-55.

82. Cochrane, 'Unsung Heroes or Muddle-Headed Peaceniks?', p. 109.

83. *Belfast Newsletter*, 3 November 2010.

84. Ibid.

85. T Paffenholz, 'Exploring opportunities and obstacles for a constructive role of social capital in peace building: a framework for analysis', Cox, *Social Capital and Peace building*, pp. 186-201, 191.

Dr Maria Power is a Lecturer in Religion and Peacebuilding at the Institute of Irish Studies, University of Liverpool. She is the author of *From Ecumenism to Community Relations: Inter-church Relations in Northern Ireland 1980–2005*,(Dublin, 2007) and editor of *Building Peace in Northern Ireland*, (Liverpool, 2011). She is currently writing a study of the Catholic Church during the conflict in Northern Ireland, focusing in particular on the work of Cardinal Cahal Daly, which will be published in 2016. Maria is also a trustee of Together for the Common Good and in her spare time works with life without parole prisoners in the United States.

This essay formed the basis of a talk at Five Leaves Bookshop in September 2014.

Also in the Five Leaves Bookshop Occasional Papers series:

#1: The Current Status of Jerusalem, by Edward Said

"I do not want to be misunderstood here. I am not arguing against peace. I have been speaking up for peace and real reconciliation between Palestinians and Israelis for over twenty years. But I do not think there can be real peace except between equals, between two peoples who together decide consciously and deliberately to share the land among themselves decently and humanely."

The Current Status of Jerusalem by Edward Said was first given as a paper in 1995 and later published in *Jerusalem Quarterly* together with an introduction by Rashid Khalidi. The essay and introduction are republished by Five Leaves Bookshop as a contribution to the current debate over the future of Israel and Palestine. Edward Said's essay is as relevant now as when it was first written.

32 pages, 978-910170-09-0

#2: Doctor Who and the Communist

Malcolm Hulke was a successful writer for radio, television and the cinema from the 1950s to the late 1970s. His work included episodes for *Armchair Theatre* and *The Avengers*, and 54 episodes for *Doctor Who*, broadcast between 1967 and 1974, for which he is best remembered. He was also a socialist, belonging for a time to the Communist Party of Great Britain, and his political views fed into his work.

Michael Herbert is a socialist historian who lives in Tameside, Greater Manchester. He teaches history to adults at Aquinas College, Stockport and Chetham's Library, Manchester. His published work includes *Never Counted Out: the story of Len*

Johnson, Manchester's Black Boxing Hero and Communist; The Wearing of the Green: a political history of the Irish in Manchester and *Up Then Brave Women: Manchester's Radical Women 1819–1918.* He is a Trustee of the Working Class Movement Library in Salford and a committee member of the Mary Quaile Club.

32 pages, 978-910170-09-0

www.fiveleavesbookshop.co.uk